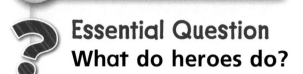

CCSS **Genre** Biography

W9-AXP-420

? **Essential Question**
What do heroes do?

Rudy Garcia-Tolson
by Ann Weil

Chapter 1

Who Is Rudy?

Rudy Garcia-Tolson was born with birth defects. He had problems with his mouth, hands, and feet. Rudy had a hard time walking.

Now Rudy is grown up. He has become a great swimmer and a hero to many people.

Jason Dewey Photography

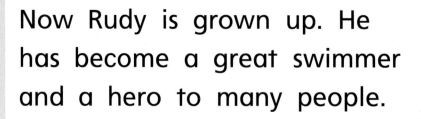

Rudy wanted to walk and play like other children. Doctors tried to fix the problems. They could not fix everything, though.

Doctors told Rudy they could give him new legs. First, they would need to take off his old legs. Rudy's family said it was all right.

Doctors help people.

When Rudy turned five years old, his legs were removed. Then the doctors gave him his new legs. The new legs were strong. They were made of plastic and metal. Now Rudy could walk and run!

This leg is like the ones that Rudy got.

STOP AND CHECK

What have you learned about Rudy so far?

4

chapter 2

What Could Rudy Do?

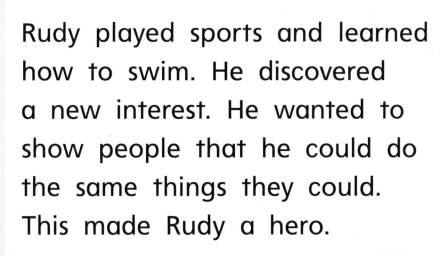

Rudy's new legs let him try new things.

Rudy played sports and learned how to swim. He discovered a new interest. He wanted to show people that he could do the same things they could. This made Rudy a hero.

Terry Martin/Rudy Garcia-Tolson

Rudy can swim fast
without legs.

Rudy loved to swim. He did not
need his new legs to swim. He
started to discover his talent. He
practiced and swam faster than
other people.

Rudy swam in races. He won
first place in many races. Other
swimmers couldn't catch him!

Rudy tried triathlons. In a triathlon, racers swim. Next they bike. Then they run. Rudy used one set of legs to bike. He used a different set to run. He became the youngest person without legs to finish a triathlon on his own.

Rudy has special legs for each sport.

Rudy swam very fast in Athens, Greece.

Rudy swam in the Paralympic Games. He won medals and set new world records. Rudy is still setting records today.

STOP AND CHECK

What new things did you learn about Rudy in this chapter?

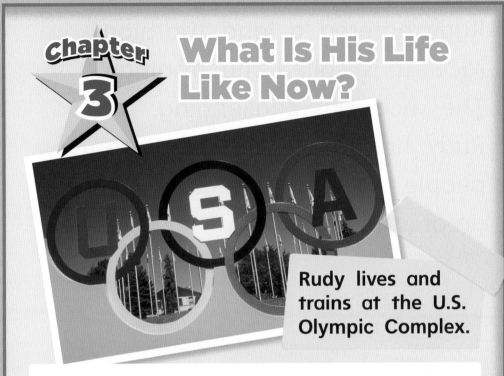

Rudy lives and trains at the U.S. Olympic Complex.

Rudy lives at a training center. He swims and trains to perform better. He spends time with other athletes. He eats healthful food. Rudy takes care of himself so he can reach his goals.

Rudy also works with doctors. The doctors study ways to make better "new legs."

Andre Jenny/Alamy

Rudy entered a long triathlon race. It is called the Ironman. The race was challenging, but Rudy finished it. He shows that people without legs can be great athletes.

Rudy puts on his legs for biking.

In 2012, Rudy trained for the Paralympic Games in London, England. He hoped to break records and win a medal.

Rudy won a gold medal at the 2008 Paralympic Games in China.

STOP AND CHECK

How does Rudy take care of himself at the training center?

Chapter 4

Why Is He a Hero?

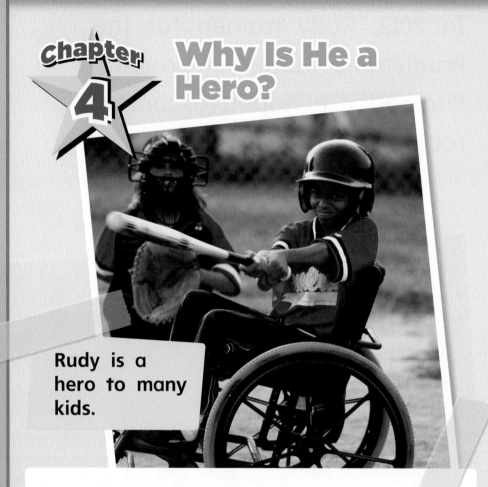

Rudy is a hero to many kids.

A hero helps others. Some heroes rescue people. Fire fighters are that kind of hero. People agree that Rudy is a different kind of hero. Rudy inspires others. He shows people how to work hard and succeed.

Ariel Skelley/CORBIS

Rudy travels to cities and shares his story with others. He tells people about his life. Rudy has a motto. A motto is a phrase that inspires people. Rudy's motto is, "A brave heart is a powerful weapon." This means that when you are not scared, you can do anything.

Rudy's success inspires others to do their best.

Rudy Garcia-Tolson

The Life of a Hero

1988 Rudy was born on September 14.

1998 At age 10, Rudy completed a triathlon.

1985 •••• 1990 •••• 1995 •••• 2000 ••••

1993 Both of Rudy's legs were removed.

2003 A magazine said Rudy was a teen who would change the world.

2004 At age 16, he won a gold medal at the Paralympic Games in Greece. He set a world record.

14

2012 His goal was to be in his third Paralympic Games.

2005 •••• 2010 •••• 2015

2007 Rudy moved to the Olympic Training Center.

2008 He won gold and bronze medals at the Paralympic Games in China.

2011 Rudy joined the U.S. team in the Pan-Pacific Para-Swimming Championships.

STOP AND CHECK

How does Rudy inspire others?

Respond to Reading

Summarize

Use details to summarize *Rudy Garcia-Tolson.*

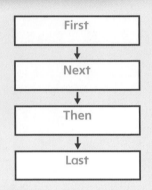

Text Evidence

1. How do you know *Rudy Garcia-Tolson* is a biography? Genre

2. What happened after Rudy turned five years old? Sequence

3. Figure out the meaning of *challenging* on page 10. Synonyms

4. Write about what Rudy did when he was 16. Write About Reading

Compare Texts
Read about another hero.

The Unsinkable Molly Brown

There is a story about a hero named Molly Brown. The story is based on a real person named Maggie Brown.

In 1912, Maggie was on a ship named the *Titanic*. It sank at sea. Many people died. About 700 survived.

Maggie Brown lived from 1867 to 1932.

Everett Collection Inc/Alamy

17

Taking Charge

Maggie was able to get into a lifeboat. Others were not so lucky. The lifeboat started to sail to safety. Maggie made the boat turn back. She wanted to help more people who were in the water.

A big ship picked up Maggie's lifeboat. Maggie was safe.

The *Titanic* sank in 1912.

The Legend

Maggie's actions made her a legend. Then someone wrote a musical about her. The writer thought *Molly* sounded better than *Maggie*. So the show was called "The Unsinkable Molly Brown."

Some things in shows about real people did not really happen that way.

Make Connections

What makes Molly a hero?
Essential Question

How is Molly like Rudy? Text to Text

Focus on
Social Studies

Purpose To identify a hero

What to Do

Step 1 ▶ Make a poster with the title "My Hero."

Step 2 ▶ Write your hero's name at the top.

Step 3 ▶ Draw pictures of two things the person did that made him or her your hero.

Step 4 ▶ Share your poster with the class.